MW00938528

MARY,

THE UNWED MOTHER OF GOD

Roger,
To my brother in Mary's Son,
may we meet again on
our way to His Kingdom —
Gonzalo T. Palacios

MARY,

THE UNWED MOTHER OF GOD

To be perfect is to have changed often,
J. H. Newman.

GONZALO T. PALACIOS

Xulon Press
2301 Lucien Way #415
Maitland, FL 32751
407.339.4217
www.xulonpress.com

© 2017 by Gonzalo T. Palacios

All rights reserved solely by the author. The author guarantees all contents are original and do not infringe upon the legal rights of any other person or work. No part of this book may be reproduced, stored in a retrieval system, or transmitted by any means without the permission of the author. The views expressed in this book are not necessarily those of the publisher.

Unless otherwise indicated, Scripture quotations taken from the Jerusalem Bible. Copyright © 1966. Used by permission.

Unless otherwise indicated, Scripture quotations taken from the Revised Standard Version (RSV). Copyright © 1946, 1952, and 1971 the Division of Christian Education of the National Council of the Churches of Christ in the United States of America. Used by permission. All rights reserved.

Cover and illustrations © Gonzalo T. Palacios

Printed in the United States of America.

ISBN-13: 9781545608050

DEDICATED TO

all my brothers and sisters in Christ and

to

all who still do not know of

our Divine kinship.

"Catholic Christendom is no simple exhibition of religious absolutism, but is presents a continuous picture of Authority and Private Judgement alternately advancing and retreating as the ebb and flow of the tide..."

John Henry Newman

Books by Gonzalo T. Palacios*

Desde Watergate hasta Chávez: diplomáticos, espias y farsantes en la capital del Imperio, Caracas, 2008 (banned in Venezuela)

From Watergate to Hugo Chávez, An ex-diplomat's memoirs, 2009

Venezuela XXI, La Revolución de la Estupidez, Bogotá, 2011

The Virgin Mary's Revolution, Love and Do What You Will, 2013

Ama y Haz lo Que Quieras, El Amor te Libera y Hace Feliz, 2015

*For copies, contact Dr. Palacios at gpgpalacios@gmail.com

TABLE OF CONTENTS:

FOREWORD

The Virgin Mary conceived Jesus out of wedlock, thus violating important regulations of the Mosaic Law (*Deuteronomy*, 23:2, 22:22, 22:28-29; *Leviticus* 20:10). Her punishment could have been death, and yet, she survived. The evangelist Luke preserved Mary's fantastic story for posterity. This book is an attempt to explain three consequences of her willingness to become the mother of Jesus:

1) Mary's submission to the will of God, her *fiat* ("let it be done") announced the end of the Mosaic Law and the beginning of the Law of Love;

2) Mary broke the regulations of the Mosaic Law concerning sexual behavior (*Matt* 1;19). The Virgin Mary's miraculous conception of Jesus revealed the primary purpose for human sexuality, i.e. to

be the manifestation of God (Love) among us ("Emmanuel"); finally,

3) Mary's physical survival ensured the restoration of humanity and Creation to their original supernatural state.

MARY → JESUS → RESURRECTION → ETERNAL LIFE

Mary, the unwed mother of God is based on two sources of unimpeachable contemporary Catholic orthodoxy: *The Catechism of the Catholic Church,* and the 2005 Encyclical *God is Love* by Pope Emeritus Benedict XVI. Other works serve to illustrate, clarify, or emphasize the veracity of the text and its adherence to Jesus' message. Thus, the subtitle, "To Be Perfect Is To Have Changed Often," is a quote from John Henry Cardinal Newman's *An Essay on the Development of Christian Doctrine.*

Gonzalo T. Palacios, PhD.   Maryland, 2017

"Wrap not yourself round in the associations of years past; nor determine that to be truth which you wish to be so, nor make an idol of cherished anticipations. Time is short, eternity long." [1]

INTRODUCTION

Two major religious faiths accept the Virgin Mary as the mother of Jesus, the son of God; Islam and Christianity. Her worldwide popularity could not be greater. Thousands have written about her spiritual significance and thousands of artists have depicted her in sculptures, paintings, and architectural masterpieces like Notre Dame in Paris and La Sagrada Familia in Barcelona, still under construction. Recently, the *National Geographic* dedicated its cover story to "Mary, The Most Powerful Woman in the World" (December 2015). And yet, the theologians are few

---

[1] John Henry Cardinal Newman, end of *An Essay on the Development of Christian Doctrine*.

that have explained what Mary's divine motherhood has meant for humanity.

Had the protagonists of Luke's story (*Luke*,1; 38) been female, or had God's proposal been made exclusively in Mary's dreams, it is unlikely that anyone – then or now - would have believed her story. The culture in which Mary was raised was *machista;* male dominated[2], a situation that persists in the 21st century.

Mary's *fiat*: submission to Power or to Authority?

The experience of *power* evolves from physical elements; the concept of *authority* develops solely in the realm of the spirit, and one is not the other.

Power relies on earthly forces and emotions derived from the application of those forces. Authority, on the other hand, is given to those who submit to wisdom, a "gift" or

---

[2] One of many examples of this culture is found in *Genesis*, 19: 8-9 in which Lot says, "Listen, I have two daughters who are virgins. I am ready to send them out to you, to treat as it pleases you. But as for the men do nothing to them, for they have come under the shadow of my roof." Clearly, hospitality to male strangers is more important to Lot than the health and happiness of his daughters.

grace that is exclusively a spiritual experience. Wisdom results from the execution of Love among humans. It is Love, i.e., God, that can transform His creatures' nature, raising it to a supernatural level of existence. The Virgin Mary's *fiat* to God's will, confirmed her supernatural existence in Eternity.

During the past half century, anthropologists claimed that we humans have one common ancestor, the African female hominin "Lucy" (1974, Ethiopia), named after the "Lucy in the sky with diamonds"[3] of the Beatles' 1967 song. While scientists have not speculated on the role Lucy may have played in the evolution of the human social order, that of the males has been studied thoroughly. They concluded that their physical strength gave the males power to control, protect, and oppress the weaker members of the tribe: children, women, and the infirm. Thus, biological factors

---

[3] "Look for the girl with the sun in her eyes," John Lennon, *Lucy in the sky with diamonds*, reminiscent of "A great sign appeared in the sky, a woman clothed with the sun, *Revelation* 12:1. https://blogs. ancientfaith.com/onbehalfofall/seeing-virgin-mary-biblical-eyes/

- Darwinian evolution - gave rise to the culture of male power, *machismo,* which survives in our day.

However, Darwinian evolution does not explain the emergence of *authority* among humans. The concept "authority" results from the use of intelligence, the ability of humans to see the "real thing" behind its appearance and to conceptualize it. The "real thing"- that which any thing *is,* now and forever - cannot be seen or perceived by physical or material means. Only the material manifestations of what the thing is can be perceived by physical senses or material instruments designed to "capture" them. For example, regardless of the changes a human body experiences throughout its temporal existence, that body manifests the same one person; *but one is not the other.* Human authority cannot be perceived by material instruments or seen by physical senses. Human authority is revealed in each person as that person co- *authors* his or her unique personality. The ability to know the reality manifesting itself presently (i.e., "now and forever") enables each person to grow in authority. Rejection of that authority means existential chaos, i.e., having no author to guide and animate one's development. In such cases, internal anarchy ensues and the individual self-destructs in due time.

The transition from the exercise of *power* to that of *authority* can be explained only when the intellect understands that transition,[4] and guides the will. All acts of understanding and of will power occur solely in the Present, *out of time and space* (the "eureka! moment, "now").

The prophet Mohammed's *Holy Qur'an* and Jesus' *New Testament,* both describe the Annunciation, undoubtedly the most significant event in the history of relations between humans and their Creator. These two scriptures were written by men and for men, reaffirming the patriarchal culture of their messengers.

For well over two thousand years, male domination has diminished the role of women in society, including

---

[4] The intellect, a spiritual instrument that uses the human brain, "reads into" (Latin, *intus+legere*) the matter the senses present to it, in order to "under-stand" or substantiate (Latin *sub+stans*) that matter.

that of the Virgin Mary. *Machismo* has informed the tenets of all major religions world-wide: it has always molded human attitudes toward their Creator and His Creation[5]. *Major religions* always attribute masculinity to God and usually promote patriarchal policies and religious beliefs. Although most religions pertain to the spiritual dimension of human existence, nonetheless they are characterized by a *machismo* which has no place in the genderless spiritual realm. In other words, the great majority of religions are built on and by the *power of men*. Christianity and Islam are no exceptions. Jesus is reported as saying, *"You are Peter, and I will build my church on this rock."*[6] If Peter is to be the foundation stone of Jesus' Church, who is her keystone? The obvious answer is that Jesus Himself provides Eternal Life to His Mystical Body, the Divine Son of the

---

[5] As in Genesis 1; 26: "Then God said, "Let us make mankind in our image, in our likeness, so that they may rule over the fish in the sea and the birds in the sky, over the livestock and all the wild animals, and over all the creatures that move along the ground."

[6] Born and raised in a patriarchal society that remains almost as *machista* today as it was then, Jesus acted according to his culture choosing a male friend to establish his Church, *Matthew* 16:18.

Virgin Mary. One problem with *machismo* is that it hinders humans[7] from developing their full potential; it prevents their "divinization".[8]

Mary's decision to accept God's proposal to become mother of His Only Begotten Son was a *fiat* that acknowledged the Father's *authority,* not His *power.* The young woman, "full of grace", was enlightened by Her Divine Lover and submitted her own will to His instead of that of Moses.

---

[7] "...true humanism[.] consists in the fact that man [...] comes to experience himself as loved by God [...] God becomes his essential happiness..." *Deus Caritas Est*, Part One, # 9.

[8] "Love is 'divine' because it comes from God, it is God, and unites us to Itself: It makes us a 'we' which transcends our divisions and makes us One, until in the end, God is 'all in all' (*1 Cor* 15:28)," in *Deus Caritas Est,* Part 1, #18.

PART I

"Blessed are the poor in spirit, for

theirs is the kingdom of heaven"

Mary's submission to the will of God, her fiat, meant freedom from the Mosaic Law, and the beginning of the Law of Love.

CHAPTER 1

Mary's submission to the will of God

"The Mosaic Law ceases to bind once its objective has been attained. The new dispensation may be called the "law of Christ" (1 *Corinthians* 9:21; *Galatians* 6:2) or the "law of the Spirit" (*Romans* 8:2)"[9].

The prophesies regarding the Virgin Mary in the Bible are too numerous to include here. New Testament texts concerning Mary comprise some 129 verses in all, scattered over seven books. Mary's own words are recorded in fifteen verses. She is explicitly given seventeen names and titles.

---

[9] Avery Cardinal Dulles, "The Covenant with Israel", in *First Things*, November 2005.

The Book of Revelation provides the most mystical descriptions of the Mother of God. More significant to Jesus' disciples, however, was her presence at Pentecost, which confirmed her as mother and foundation of the Church:

> "When they entered the city, they went to the upper room where they were staying, Peter and John and James and Andrew, Philip and Thomas, Bartholomew and Matthew, James son of Alpheus, Simon the Zealot, and Judas son of James. All these devoted themselves with one accord to prayer, *together with some women, and Mary the mother of Jesus, and his brothers...*" (*Acts* 1:13-15).

The Holy Quran also mentions Mary[10] and accepts her Divine maternity:

> "O Mary! Verily, Allah gives you the glad tidings of a Word [*'Be' and he was! Jesus*

---

[10] Surahs #42, 43, 45, 47 in the Holy Quran.

the Son of Mary] from Him, his name will be the Messiah. Jesus the son of Mary, held in honor in this world and hereafter, and will be one of those near to Allah." Surah 45.

Prophetic credibility.

The importance and credibility of a prophecy can be evaluated by its consequences on the community to which it is addressed. The role of Mary in the history of humanity was prophesied from the earliest biblical writings (*Genesis* 3:15). Some prophets provide very specific information regarding the mother of the Messiah. For example, some 700 years before the Virgin Mary was born, the prophet Isaiah proclaimed that the mother of the Jewish Messiah would be a virgin (*Isaiah*, 7:14). Twenty-one centuries ago, Mary, adolescent, virginal, and unmarried, became the person announced by various prophets throughout the history of the people of Israel.

5

True and false prophets have influenced the religions of the world. Soon after a religious movement begins, its followers often attribute the gift of prophesy to their founder. Various writings of two of the World's greatest thinkers, Buddha and Plato seem to prepare humanity for Mary's message of submission to her Omnipotent Love, God,[11] although neither thinker was familiar with her Jewish culture. Centuries later, a pubescent girl in Nazareth would put aside her own tradition and break with its religious laws, claiming to have received a message from her God. The same God who had given the Laws to Moses and the prophets, had impregnated her. Who would believe her fantastic story?[12]

---

[11] For Plato, see his *Symposium*. The Buddha preached "*sila*", an ethic based on love and compassion, foreshadowing that of Mary's Son: see *L'enseignement du Bouddha d'après les textes les plus anciens,* by Walpola Rahula, du Seuil, Paris, 1961; pages 72 and 130-131, "L'Amour Universel".

[12] Or, as G. K. Chesterton expressed it, "the strangest story in the world," *The Everlasting Man*, Dover Publications, 2007, page 262.

"Jesus is only able to speak about the Father in the way he does because he is the Son, because of his filial communion with the Father."[13]

CHAPTER 2

Mary's Fantastic Story

"...the Word of God becomes her word, and her word issues from the Word of God."[14]

The apostle Luke reported the Virgin Mary's fantastic story in his gospel (*Luke* 1; 26-38). To whom was the announcement made? Was it to the girl possessed by Love (God)? Was God addressing the people of Israel once more? Or was it to the world at large? The historical consequences of the Annunciation indicate the message was intended to all three. And in the context of these three interlocutors, the

---

[13] Pope Benedict XVI, *Jesus of Nazareth*, Ignatius, San Francisco, 2007, page 7.

[14] Pope Benedict XVI, *Deus Caritas Est*, Part 2, # 41.

adjective "fantastic" aptly describes the story Mary allegedly told her family and friends to justify her pregnancy.[15]

From the earliest days of Christianity, the event was dubbed "The Annunciation," referring to the Archangel Gabriel's announcing God's incarnation. Luke reported Mary's dialog with the Divine messenger in these words:

> "...the angel Gabriel was sent by God to a town in Galilee called Nazareth, to a virgin betrothed to a man named Joseph, of the House of David.
>
> He went and said to her, 'Rejoice, you who enjoy God's favor! The Lord is with you'. She was deeply disturbed by these words and asked herself what this greeting could mean, but the angel said to her, 'Mary,

---

[15] "Mary is unmarried when the angel comes. The angel's invitation and her independent decision tell us Mary does not need permission of clergy – or her parents – to become pregnant. God knows Mary owns her own body. And there is no shame in her decision. Mary is good news for unwed mothers everywhere." Nancy Rockwell, "No More Lying about Mary", in *Patheos*, 12/03/2016.

do not be afraid; you have won God's favor.
Look! You are to conceive in your womb
and bear a son, and you must name him
Jesus. He will be great and will be called the
Son of the Most High. The Lord God will
give him the throne of his ancestor David;
he will rule over the House of Jacob forever
and his reign will have no end.'

Mary said to the angel, 'But how can
this come about, since I have no knowledge
of man?' The angel answered, 'The Holy
Spirit will come upon you, and the power
of the Most High will cover you with its
shadow. And so, the child will be holy and
will be called the Son of God. And I tell you
this too: your cousin Elizabeth also, in her
old age, has conceived a son, and she whom
people called barren, is now in her sixth
month, for nothing is impossible to God.'

> Mary said, 'You see before you the Lord's
>
> servant, let it happen to me as you have said.'
>
> And the angel left her." *Luke 1, 26-38*.

Why was Mary's story "fantastic"? Not because it was a fantasy of her youthful imagination: on the contrary, since she "knew no man", Mary could not fantasize becoming pregnant. The ultimate meaning of Mary's pregnancy story would bes revealed by her Son shortly before he died, namely, that Mary was the new Eve:

> "Seeing his mother and the disciple he loved
>
> standing near her, Jesus said to his mother,
>
> 'Woman, this is your son.'" (*John*: 19, 26)

Jesus died and immediately prepared a place in his Father's kingdom for *all* humanity, including those at the foot of His cross, the thief dying next to him ("...today you will be with me in Paradise." *Luke* 23, 43), and all who had left this world (Ac 2: 24, Mt 12:40 and Mt 16:18). After all,

He had already promised us: "I shall return to take you with me; so, that where *I am* you may be too.[16]

"...But He takes a body of our kind, and not merely so, but from a spotless and stainless virgin, knowing not a man, a body clean and in very truth pure from intercourse of men. For being Himself mighty, and Artificer of everything, He prepares the body in the Virgin as a temple unto Himself, and makes it His very own as an instrument, in it manifested, and in it dwelling." Athanasius, *On the Incarnation of the Word*.

CHAPTER 3:

Erotic Love and the Virgin Mary's *Fiat*

God loves, and his love may certainly be called *Eros,* yet it is also totally *agape*.[17]

Mary's *fiat* entailed a rejection of essential segments of the Mosaic Law[18]. Her submission to Love's will, "let it happen to me as you have said," also announces the New Law of Love, the Law of Christ. From

---

[17]Benedict XVI, *Deus Caritas Est*, Part One, No. 9; the Pope referred to Ps-Dionysius the Areopagite, *The Divine Names*, IV, 12-14.

[18]As in *Leviticus* 20:10, *Deuteronomy* 22:28-29, and *Exodus* 22: 16-17.

that moment, the Mosaic Covenant was to be re-interpreted in a new light, the Light of her Son Jesus, already alive in her womb[19]. Two thousand years later, Avery Cardinal Dulles claimed that "The Mosaic Law ceases to bind once its objective has been attained," which had been taught from the earliest days of the Church (1 *Corinthians* 9:21; *Galatians* 6:2, *Romans* 8:2)[20].

The incarnation of *human beings*, then and now, may result from sexual intercourse. Mary's story, however, is that the incarnation of her Son resulted purely from her Divine Lover's omnipotent spiritual creative energy[21]. Luke's account of the Annunciation ends with the angel leaving her. Mary's Divine Lover, however, remained

---

[19]"The Virgin shall conceive and give birth to a son and they will call him Emmanuel, which means 'God is with us'."

[20]"The Covenant with Israel", Avery Cardinal Dulles, in *First Things*, November 2005.

[21]The messenger's explanation to Mary was: "The Holy Spirit will come upon you and the power of the Most High will cover you with its shadow. And so the child will be holy and will be called the Son of God."

within her, present in her womb as "the only begotten Son of God."[22] In the words of Athanasius,

> "And this was the wonderful thing that He was at once walking as man, and as the Word was quickening all things, and as the Son was dwelling with His Father. So, that not even when the Virgin bore Him did He suffer any change, nor by being in the body was [His glory] dulled: but, on the contrary, He sanctified the body also."[23]

Eros becomes *agape.*

Mary's *fiat* also revealed the Father's purpose of human sexuality within the context of the new Law of Christ, Love Incarnate, where *eros* becomes *agape*. This revelation has

---

[22] Nicene Creed.

[23] "St. Athanasius wrote this text in the 4th century, his style is easy to follow and his concepts are of irreplaceable worth", Emmalon Davis: *How the Incarnation did not limit the ubiquity of the Word, nor diminish His Purity. (Simile of the Sun.)*, # 17: 5. https://www.ccel.org/ccel/athanasius/incarnation.html

not been universally accepted by her Son's disciples. When Mary submitted to Love's will rather than to her own, she chose to ignore the Mosaic Law, regardless of the consequences. When she became the unwed mother of her Love-Child, she freed herself, by the power of the Holy Spirit, from the Old Covenant. Mary could not have given her *fiat* unless an act of Divine Love (*agape*) illuminated her. An act of Divine Love (*agape*, in Eternity) that took place in her body (*eros*). Her Divine Lover is present physically inside her; a true and efficient description of erotic love.[24] ,

Through Mary, *with* her, and *in* her, the Father of her Divine Son, revealed that *the reproduction of His image* (mankind) *has nothing to do with human sexuality.*[25] Thanks to God the Father, Mary's Divine Motherhood

---

[24] "God loves, and his love may certainly be called *eros*, yet it is also totally called *agape*:" *Deus Caritas Est*, Part One, # 9. Pope Benedict XVI refers the readers to Ps.-Dionysius the Areopagite who calls God both *eros* and *agape* in his treatise *The Divine Names*.

[25] "*Genesis* 1, 27: "God created man (mankind) in the image of himself, in the image of God he created him (them); male and female he created them."

restored humans to their original *supernatural* state rather than being mere products of *natural* evolution[26]:

> "... we were as good as slaves to the elemental principles of this world, but when the appointed time came, God sent His Son, born of a woman, born a subject of the Law, to redeem the subjects of the Law and to enable us to be adopted as sons."
>
> *Galatians*, 4, 3-6.

Just as Adam and Eve were created without sexual (human) intervention, the New Adam was created directly by God. The New Eve, Mary, was conceived by unknown human parents, but, like the first Eve, also free of sin. *Through* Mary, *with* her, and *in* her, human sexuality proclaims and manifests the glory of Love, the Father of her Son, of His brothers and sisters, and of the New Eve and her progeny.

---

[26] Aristotle's "rational animals", in *De Anima*, III, 4-11.

"And if we are children, then we are heirs:
heirs of God and co-heirs with Christ--if
indeed we suffer with Him, so that we may
also be glorified with Him." *Romans* 8:17.

"Male and female he created them:" through the centuries, the word "man" has been translated more properly as "mankind". The attribution of gender to the Creator ("himself." "he") is undoubtedly due to the *machista* culture mentioned in the Introduction. The exclusively male image of God is not applicable to the children of God. Were that case, the Virgin Mary would not "have won God's favor" and thus become Θεοτόκος, Theotokos, the Mother of God.

"[Conjugal love], merging the human with the divine…is uniquely expressed and perfected through the maritalact." *The Church Today*, II,1, 49.

CHAPTER 4:

The Sexuality of the Children of Love

"Let him kiss me with the kisses of his mouth. Your love-making is more delightful than wine…"

Song of Solomon.

Thanks to two instruments of the soul, intelligence and free will, humans learn the natural law as it is written in their hearts[27]. "Human law," as Dante called it, "is above mere animal instinct and certainly above bestiality."[28] The Virgin Mary's consent to the request of God's Love, elevated

---

[27] "…the permanent binding force of universal natural law and its all-embracing principles…" *Pastoral Constitution on the Church in the Modern World*, Chapter V, Section1, # 79, Pope Paul VI, 12/07/1965.

[28] See note # 29.

human law to "divine law"; from natural law to supernatural law. Mary's *fiat* asserted the divine origin of human beings; the children of God with the "New Eve." Along with Love's only begotten Son, all humans would also be Fathered by the Virgin Mary's Divine Lover. God's paternal love explains the "Our" in Our Lord's prayer. Mary's miraculous maternity restored the original divine filiation of humanity.

Two Myths about Divine and Human Law.

In his *Divina Commedia*, Dante mentions the chastity of Mary, the Mother of God, and that of Diana in Roman mythology, as examples of "a divine law."[29] In the first instance, the poet quotes the Virgin's words, "*Virum non cognosco*" (I know no man), addressed to her Divine Lover's messenger. On the other hand, Diana is praised for protecting her chastity, by the souls Dante places in Purgatory. The two stories, one from Saint Luke's gospel

---

[29] *Purgatorio*, canto XXV, 127-132; see Note 27.

and the other from Roman mythology, are examples of the "divine law" underlying Dante's *Divine Comedy*.

Diana's myth parallels Mary's in several ways. Although Mary eventually married Joseph, the stories have it that both women remained virginal their entire lives. Their virginity symbolized fertility; Mary became the "New Eve", the mother of the New Adam and the succeeding humanity, while Diana was worshipped by pregnant women seeking the healthy delivery of their children. Mary's love and care for infants and for the unborn is well documented in the New Testament (for instance, Mary's visit to her cousin). Diana was revered by the Roman lower classes, which can also be said of the Virgin Mary's concern for the poor and powerless of the world.[30]

The Virgin Mary's *Fiat* and Erotic Love.

"Sexuality, in which man's belonging to the bodily and biological world is expressed, becomes personal and truly

---

[30]As seen in the Virgin Mary's dealing with the servants at Cana, with her son Jesus, and confirmed repeatedly in her apparitions to children at Lourdes, Fatima, and to Juan Diego in Guadalupe.

human when it is integrated into the relationship of one person to another, in the complete and lifelong mutual gift of a man and a woman."[31]

Clearly, the last five words of *C.C.C.* # 2337 introduce gender into the sexual relationship. These five words contradict the genderless opening sentence of this numeral, which affirms that "Charity means the successful integration of sexuality within the *person* and thus the inner unity of man in his bodily and spiritual being." Numeral 2337 deals with "The Vocation to Chastity": it closes with the affirmation that "The virtue of chastity therefore involves the integrity of the *person* and the integrity of the gift," both of which are genderless.

The "inner unity" mentioned here alludes to each human being, male or female, and not just to "*man* in *his* bodily and spiritual being." The term "person" is more accurate, as

---

[31]*C.C.C.*# 2337. The English and the Spanish translations of the Catechism use the terms "man" and "hombre" in this and other numerals, referring to human beings or persons. This usage can be attributed to the culture of male predominance mentioned earlier in the Introduction. This practice creates confusion and promotes error.

in "the integration of sexuality within the *person*," and later, in "chastity therefore involves the integrity of the *person*."

Regardless of one's sexuality, each "human person," body and soul, is created in our (genderless) Creator's image. By the Power of the Father's Love, i.e., the Holy Spirit, the *Virgin* Mary gave birth to their Son Jesus. Simply said, the Incarnation was a miraculous act of Divine Love, in which Mary's sexuality played no role. She revealed to us by her *fiat* that "the challenge of *eros* can be said to be truly overcome when this unification (body and soul) is achieved."[32] The Mother of God did not "achieve" this unification: The Virgin Mary was conceived thus "unified".

"Divine Law" and Mary's sexuality.

Guided by Jesus' command to love one another (*John* 13, 34), our sexual life should,

"by its very nature be joyous, uncon-
strained, alive, leisurely, inventive, and

---

[32] Benedict XVI, *Deus Caritas Est*, Introduction, # 5.

full of a special delight which the lovers
have learned by experience to create for
one another. There is no more beautiful
gift of God than the little secret world of
creative love and expression in which two
persons who have totally surrendered to
each other manifest and celebrate their
mutual gift. *It is precisely in this spirit of
celebration, gratitude, and joy that true
purity is found.* The pure heart is not one
that is terrified of *eros* but one that, with
the confidence and abandon of a child of
God, accepts this gift as a sacred trust, for
sex, too, is one of the talents Christ has
left us to trade with uuntil He returns.[33]"

---

[33] "Nostro peccato fu ermafrodito;/ma perché non servammo umana legge,/ seguendo come bestie l'appetito,/in obbrobrio di noi", *Purg.* 26.82- 87). In this canto, Dante reinforces Merton's words, where he defies expectations in two key ways in his construction of human sexuality: 1) Dante reclassifies homosexuality as he moves [it] from Hell (where it is a sin of violence against nature, *Inferno* 15-16) to Purgatory where it is a form of lust and therefore of incontinence. In this way *homosexuality becomes a variant of human sexual*

(Thomas Merton, *Love and Living*, 1981.)

Merton's words evoke *The Song of Songs* and Pope Benedict XVI's *Deus Caritas Est*, to mention only two references to divinized human sexuality in the Christian context. We are images of God, and *God is Love*.[34] Our lives should proclaim the joy of "God-is-with-us," and that we are one in Jesus. Within the Sacrament of Marriage, Merton discovers the "special delight." That of Oneness in Love, inhuman sexual acts.[35] For instance, when ecstasy is reached in simultaneous sexual orgasm, the act is the physiological symbol of three persons in One: man, wife, and Love Incarnate.

---

behavior, akin to heterosexuality. As a form of human sexuality, it can be excessive, and hence require purgation; *the implication is that it can also be not excessive.* Here Dante appears tolerant and progressive from a modern perspective; 2) He criminalizes heterosexual excess…" ITALICS ADDED.THE DIVINE COMEDY BY DANTE ALIGHIERI· DIGITAL DANTE EDITION WITH COMMENT· MMXV · COLUMBIA UNIVERSITY.

[34] See Pope Benedict XVI's Encyclical (Rome, 2005) by that name.

[35] "Through this union [conjugal love] they experience the meaning of their oneness, and attain to it with growing perfection day by day," *The Church Today*, II, 1, 48.

The instant Mary conceived, God interjected Himself into His creature: The *Eternal* Father begat in His *temporal* Creation. When Jesus was conceived, "life" no longer referred to the product of biological evolution alone. God's incarnation took place in "the fullness of time," in the Present. From that moment forward, when applied to humans, a.k.a. the *Mystical Body of Christ*, the term "life," no longer meant an accidental biological occurrence. *In*, *through*, and *with* Mary, God's Son revealed to us the real meaning of "Life":

NOTHING BUT A WILLING VEHICLE WITH A HUMAN MOTHER'S CONCERNS.

- "I am the way and the truth and the life;"

- "In him was life, and that life was the light of men;

- "Jesus said to her, 'I am the resurrection and the life. He who believes in me will live, even though he dies;'"

- "…his Son Jesus Christ. He is the true God and eternal life." (John 14, 6; 11, 25; 5, 20 respectively).

25

Mary's *fiat* exposed the spiritual nature of human exis-tence. To lead a fully human "life" now means to let Jesus animate one's life, or in Mary's words, "Do whatever he tells you." Once we assent to do God's will and abandon all things, including one's "flesh", then we may enter the kingdom of God and gain *eternal* life. Eternal Life, not merely temporal existence. Spiritual Life, not merely physical: "He who believes in me will live [in the Spirit], even though he dies".

In sum, in the Virgin Mary's story, the Law of Love, God, had replaced that of Moses. She had accepted to pro-mulgate the New Law, that of her Son Jesus.

"My Mother and my brothers are those who
hear the word of God and put it into practice."
Luke 8:20.

Chapter 5:

The Primary End of the Family

"He who loves father or mother more than me
is not worthy of me; and he who loves son or
daughter more than me is not worthy of me."
Mt 10:37.

Mary's *fiat* not only initiated the New Covenant, but by consenting to be the mother of "the Only Begotten Son of God", she became a special member of the Holy Trinity. The Trinity is now the Virgin Mary's Holy Family. Moments before His death on the cross, Jesus declared the apostle John His Mother's son, making "all who hear the word of God and put it into practice" His family. The primary end of the family, of *all* families, is to hear and incarnate the Word of God. The end or goal of a family is the reproduction of Love (God) among us;

an invisible, spiritual Person. The reproduction of the biological parents or of their potential offspring is not what defines a Christian family[36].

C.C.C. # 2361 reiterates the Virgin Mary's story and Jesus' words:[37]

"Sexuality [...] is not something merely biological, but concerns the innermost being of the human person as such. It is realized in a truly human way only if it is an integral part of the love by which a man and a woman commit themselves totally to one another until death."[38]

---

[36] "The procreation of children is not essential to marriage. Matrimony, in all its essentials, is had even though no children result from the union;" Leo J. Latz, The Rhythm...in Women, Latz Foundation, Chicago, 1942, page 122.

[37] *Mt.* 10:37 and *Luke* 8:20, quoted earlier.

[38] The Catechism quotes St. John Paul II's encyclical *Familiaris Consortio*, 11.

Mary's submission to "the power of the Most High" implied abandoning the old Mosaic Laws. "You see before you the Lord's servant, let it happen to me as you have said;" not as Moses had commanded[39]. At the same time, the Blessed Mother's answer to God's messenger, proclaimed the new Law of Christ, of Love personified. Eventually, Mother and Son, by the power of the Holy Spirit, would deliver the Father's "kingdom," and the Virgin Mary's actions would restore humanity to its original supernatural dimension.

There are other references in the *Catechism* affirming Jesus' message regarding the ultimate reason for erotic manifestations of Love, namely, to do the will of Our Father. A clearer understanding of the Divine Will of Love is obtained, when the phrase "procreation of life" is understood as the procreation of Jesus, of "God-is- with-us," as

---

[39] For instance, *Matthew* 10:37 quoted earlier ("He who loves father or mother more than me ...") subjects the Fourth Commandment to the First, where Jesus identifies Himself ("me") with "the Lord Your God."

was announced to the Virgin Mary. The *Catechism* states in Numeral #2367 that,

> "Called to give life, spouses share in the creative power and fatherhood of God. 'Married couples should regard it as their proper mission to transmit human life and to educate their children;
>
> > they should realize that they are thereby *cooperating with* the love of *God, the Creator*, and are, in a certain sense, its interpreters. They will fulfill this duty with a sense of human and Christian responsibility.'" (Paul VI, *Gaudium et Spes,* # 50).

The sharing in "the creative power and fatherhood of God," as Pope Paul VI wrote, does not refer to the reproduction of "the flesh", but rather, of the incarnation of Love. Contrary to "traditional" interpretation, "cooperating with the love of God" emphasizes the spiritual significance Jesus gave to the word "Life". In the context of Jesus' New Law of Love, the terms "human," "transmit human life," and "life," imply an intimate, loving relationship with God the Father[40]:

"I give you a new commandment: love one another; just as I have loved you, you also must love one another. By this love you have for one another, everyone will know that you are my disciples." (*John* 13, 34).

Benedict XVI reaffirms the spiritual unity of love between God and man in *God is Love*,

"Fundamentally, 'love' is a single reality, but with different dimensions [...] Yet, when the two dimensions are totally cut off from one another, the result is a caricature or at least an impoverished form of love."[41]

---

[40] "...the Fathers of the Church saw this inseparable connection between ascending and descending love, between *Eros* which seeks God and *Agape* which passes on the gift received symbolized in various ways." Benedict XVI, *God is Love*, Part One, #7: a spiritual relationship.

[41] *God is Love*, Part One, #8.

In the New Covenant, human sexuality refers to "the capacity to love and to procreate" and "forming bonds of communion with others," not physically but spiritually (*C.C.C* # 2332). In Christ, there is no gender, "there is neither male nor female." (*Galatians* 3, 28). The capacity to love, to procreate, and to form bonds of communion with others, are *spiritual* activities, not those of the flesh.

In Christ, sexuality is elevated to a supernatural level. If intentionally devoid of their supernatural content, mere animal or biological sexual activities degrade the New Adam. On the other hand, sexual acts referring to human and Divine *interpersonal* relationships manifest God's presence among us. In the Virgin Mary's story, the only begotten Son of God [...] was conceived by the Holy Spirit in the person of the Virgin Mary, and the Second Person of God[42] became man." Mary's conception and Jesus' birth revealed that supernatural human procreation depends *entirely* on God the Father. Physical or biological sexuality

---

[42] "born of the Father before all ages;" Nicene Creed.

has no other reason to be than to *joyfully* manifest the glory of Love (God), *offspring or not.*

Sexuality, Marriage, Pleasure and Enjoyment.

It is a constant in the evolution of primates and other mammals, that their sexuality developed closely linked to their physiological and biological characteristics. Physical strength and intuition are means by which animals relate to one another. Thousands of years after human intelligence appeared on Earth[43], thanks to Our Lady and to her Divine Lover, it was revealed that "Sexuality [...] is not something merely biological, but concerns the innermost being of the human *person* as such."[44]

The concept of "complementary" sexuality is mentioned explicitly in *C.C.C. #* 372 and *#* 2333, as both numerals reduce sexuality to its biological dimension and

---

[43] Biological Evolution of itself does not explain Human Intelligence.

[44] C.C.C., # 2361. Words not included in the quote: "by means of which man and woman give themselves to one another through the acts which are proper and exclusive to spouses".

transmission of physical life between two people. In *C.C.C.* # 372 and # 2333, "complementarity" means nothing more than a grammatical distinction and a way of harmonizing the physiological needs of the couple, and of society at large. Ironically, *C.C.C.* # 2333 opens with the ambivalent phrase: "Man and woman were made 'for each other'", and continues with, "not that God left them half made and incomplete". However, the validity of *complementarity* depends on God's "leaving them half made and incomplete."

Another serious issue with the concept complementarity is that it finds no parallel in, nor explanation for, the Virgin Mother's sexuality, which, as the same *C.C.C.* # 2333 explains, should be acknowledged by "Everyone, man and woman." No one "complemented" Mary, the unwed Mother of God.

Mary, the Unwed Mother of God does not explain logical contradictions regarding human sexuality. Through the centuries the Church, under the guise of the Magisterium and Tradition, has misinterpreted evolutionary outcomes, such as "complementary sexuality"[45]. The following pages attempt to analyze Mary's role in understanding that God's *eros* is also totally *agape*.[46]

Errors regarding love and sexuality include:

- not acknowledging that the Virgin Mary's *fiat* is the start of the New Covenant and the end of the Old Covenant;

- ignoring Jesus' New Law: "I give a new you a new commandment: love one another; just as I have loved you, you also must love one another (*John* 13: 34-35)"; and,

- reducing human sexuality to a mere animal or bio-logical activity.

C.C.C. #2360 and #2361 explain that in the *sacrament* of marriage, "a man and a woman give themselves to one

---

[45] Examples of erroneous concepts in the Catechism: "complementarity" (# 2333); "Sexuality is ordered to the conjugal love of man and woman" (# 2360); [human] "life" (# 2366, # 2367); "end of marriage" (#2366, #2367).

[46] *Deus Caritas Est*, I, # 10.

another." The emphasis on the physical/biological dimension of this gift from God is achieved by conditioning the giving by each gender. Marriage, defined in these terms, is equivalent to a natural contract or relationship that may not necessarily attain the status of *sacrament*. Marriages defined solely by the biological characteristics of the ministers of the sacrament[47] are not valid; for a marriage contract to become a sacrament, the Holy Spirit must come upon the couple and "the power of the Most High will cover [them] with its shadow"[48]; this was announced to Mary at the start of the New Covenant.

C.C.C. # 1116 succinctly defines what the sacraments of the New Law are:

"Sacraments are powers that come forth from the Body of Christ, which is ever-living and life-giving. They are actions of the Holy Spirit, at work in his Body, the Church.

---

[47] The couple getting married are the ministers of the sacrament of Matrimony.

[48] Biological characteristics of the couple are not a reliable sign of the presence of the Holy Spirit among them.

They are "the masterworks of God" in the New and everlasting Covenant."

To define the Sacrament of Marriage in terms of accidental qualities like gender (# 2334), or as "a way of *imitating in the flesh* [!] the Creator's generosity and fecundity" (# 2335), or even in terms of sexuality alone (#2360), borders on heresy. The "powers that come forth from the Body of Christ" are not of this world. Through the sacraments, we receive supernatural, ever-living Life, nourished by Jesus Christ Himself.

In the Sacrament of Marriage, Jesus provides us with the "powers that come forth" from His Love: "God's way of loving becomes the measure of human love."[49] The Sacrament of Marriage is the *essential* union of two *complete* human beings, whose will to become one is energized by the Holy Spirit. It is God, the Omnipotent Love, Who replicates Itself in the Sacrament of Holy Matrimony (as He did in Mary's

---

[49] *God is Love, # 11.*

womb): creating One out of three, the two ministers *and* the Spirit of Jesus.

Conditioning the Sacrament to biological powers can be compared to defining the supernatural reality of the Eucharist in terms of the natural material components of the wafer and the wine used in the Sacrament. Just as the faithful believe that the Sacrament of the Eucharist is not a mere remembrance of Jesus' presence on Earth or an imitation of the Last Supper, the ministers of the Sacrament of Marriage should believe that their "intimate partnership of life and love…is rooted in their irrevocable personal consent" to have Our Lord Present in their union (*C.C.C.* # 2364). Those who administer the Sacrament of Marriage, should believe in its efficacy as a direct channel of God's grace, and not as "a way of *imitating in the flesh* (# 2335)" any of God's attributes.

Despite the frequent materialistic wording of many of the numerals dedicated to marriage and the family, the *Catechism* does reiterate the spiritual and supernatural dimension of human sexuality: "it is realized in a truly human way *only* if it is an integral part of the love...."

The Slow Death of the Old Covenant.

C.C.C. #2367 also interprets human sexuality in a materialistic or merely natural way, i.e. physical procreation of children. The origins of this materialistic and erroneous interpretation of human sexuality is found in the *Catechism* itself. In it, there is a *quasi-idolatrous* adherence to "Its principal sources [which] are the Sacred Scriptures, the Fathers of the Church, the liturgy, and the Church's Magisterium."[50]

However, the procreation of children, to which *The Catechism* refers, is "not something simply biological," as Pope John Paul II wrote in *Familiaris Consortio*. The "creative power and fatherhood of God" are not revealed in the evolutionary process, but in *the Eternal Present ("the fullness of time"), in which all acts of God's Love occur.* "Cooperating with the love of God the Creator" is not a

---

[50] Pope John Paul II, *Catechism of the Catholic Church*, Prologue, III, 11.

material, physical enterprise, but rather, another aspect of the single reality that is Love. Married couples, single persons, consecrated virgins, celibate persons, heterosexual and homosexual couples and individuals, *in sum, all of us, have the obligation to regard our "proper mission to transmit human life," which we know by faith to be the life of Christ,* not necessarily that of any one man or woman.

Sexual intercourse may or may not bring another member of Jesus' Mystical Body into the world. The miracle of Life, both natural and supernatural, is beyond the power of humanity. To pretend otherwise is to pretend to "be like gods" and to be immortal[51], a grace that was restored to us through the New Eve, the Virgin Mary, "You see before you the Lord's servant, let it happen to me as you have said."

---

[51] See *Genesis*, 3.

"Husband and wife, therefore, by seeking and enjoying this pleasure do no wrong whatever."
Pius XII, Address to Midwives,
October 29, 1951.

CHAPTER 6:

Sexual Pleasure, a Gift from Love, Our Father.

"As a youth, I had been woefully at fault, particularly in early adolescence. I had prayed to you for chastity and said 'Give me chastity and continence, but not yet.' For I was afraid that you would answer my prayer at once and cure me too soon of the disease of lust, which I wanted satisfied, not quelled." (St. Augustine, *Confessions* VIII, 7).

Two important facts must be kept in mind regarding Augustine's prayer for chastity. First, recently, science demonstrated the physiological effects of testosterone "in early adolescence" among males. It is feasible that today, an adolescent Augustine would be more understanding of

41

his *natural* tendencies[52] and not consider himself "woefully at fault." Second, the future Doctor of the Church was not ready for chastity for another reason: for many years, he had been a convinced Manichean. According to Manes, both Good and Evil were equal supernatural divinities. As such, the "disease of lust" was a powerful force of Evil in his life. That force was opposed by the virtue of chastity, the balancing energy of Good.

Having overcome his Manichean past, after his conversion to Christianity, Saint Augustine would explain in his *Confessions* that lust was a *spiritual* affliction. That affliction has physical consequences other than the ephemeral pleasures derived from satisfying sensual appetites.

> "Many years of my life had passed— twelve, unless I am wrong— since I had read Cicero's *Hortensius* at the age of nineteen and it had inspired me to study philosophy. But I still postponed my renunciation of this world's joys..." (St. Augustine, *Confessions, loc. cit.*).

---

[52] Christopher West's "vertical wildness" comes to mind: "Letting good things run wild is what I call 'vertical wildness.' We have wild desires in us because we're made to 'go wild' with God, in God;" *Fill These Hearts*, page 47.

The First General Anesthesia.

"God made the man fall into a deep sleep." Then, from one of Adam's ribs, He created his "helpmate", Eve. The Divine Surgeon inflicted no pain to either of his creations. Naked, the couple enjoyed a harmonious coexistence with the animals, plants, and the rest of the Cosmos. The Creator made only one request to them which would not diminish any of their pleasures on Earth. And yet, Adam and Eve disobeyed. Immediately, the characteristics they shared with the rest of the animals around them, replaced the preternatural gifts with which they had been created. Adam and Eve lost their innocence in regards to their bodies and instead of enjoying the beauty of their Creator's image, they only saw their physical nakedness. The most significant preternatural gift they lost was *immortality*: they were expelled from God's Garden. Before their disobedience, The Lord kept them in His Presence, not at a distance. Jesus Christ, the New Adam, explained how we could return to Eden: Repent, acknowledge your sins, and trust in His merciful arms.

As Jesus told it, the parable of the Prodigal Son presupposes that the Father had forgiven the young man before his return. It also means that the son *is* indeed the offspring of the generous Old Man. Jesus also revealed the role His mother was to play in the Redemption drama: the New Eve, mother of The New Adam, restored humanity to Our Father's family.

Nineteen centuries have not been enough for Christians to understand the differences between the concepts of Authority and Power. One blatant example was Pope Paul VI's 1968 encyclical *Humanae vitae*. Pope Paul VI intended to end further discussions on all forms of birth control, an issue that the hierarchy of the Church has managed through the centuries. In fact, Pope Paul VI only succeeded in stirring the controversy worldwide. The encyclical was not so much about sexual practices as it was about papal power to control the faithful. The teachings in *Humanae vitae* were given as infallible pronouncements by the authority of Saint Peter's successor. In fact, the main motivation for the encyclical was to preserve the appearance that the teachings of the Church never change. Today, half a century later, the hierarchy of the Church is still seeking the guidance of the Holy Spirit regarding human sexuality. Two thousand years ago, the Virgin Mary revealed that "nothing is impossible for God" and that sexual acts are meant to joyfully manifest Love among humans. Only Love gives supernatural Life.

Sexual Pleasure, a Gift from Love.

Christians take pleasure in exhibiting God's love for humanity. Mary was the first example of this pleasure when she shared her "good news" with her cousin Elizabeth. The pleasure itself was not from a sexual experience, but it certainly was erotic in the highest form. Divine Love – agape – is incarnate in Mary's womb – eros. Mary's joy and pleasure inspired her to say

> "My soul proclaims the greatness of the Lord
> And my spirit exults in God my Savior;
> because He has looked upon this lowly
> handmaid. Yes, from this day forward all

generations will call me blessed, for the

Almighty has done great things for me…"

(*Luke* 1: 46-49)

It is no contradiction of Saint Joseph's manly holiness that he decided to divorce Mary when she was found to be with child. The important words of the Bible are that he planned to do this "quietly", because he was "a righteous man, yet unwilling to expose her to shame" (*Matthew* 1:19).

CHAPTER 7:

This World's Joys.

"The curve of your thighs is like the curve of a necklace, work of a master hand. Your navel..." *Song of Songs,* 7: 2.

I t is right and just to end this part of *Mary, the Unwed Mother of God,* recapitulating the steps that bring us "the joys of this world," to use Saint Augustine's words. By her *fiat,* Our Blessed Mother, began the Eternal ("born of the Father before all ages") restoration of humans to their original supernatural status. Among the signs of that restored status, Our Father reinstated the preternatural gift of immortality:[53] we "look forward to the resurrection of the dead and the life of the world to come."

At the same time, Mary's actions ended the Old Covenant[54], its rules and laws, designed to control, discipline, and subjugate the followers of Moses. Mary's acceptance of God's request that she be His Son's mother, was itself a proclamation of the freedom obtained by our Messiah. Mary also started the New Covenant, which her Son would implement later. The New Eve gave birth to the New Adam, a.k.a. the Mystical Body of the Only Begotten Son of God. The new humanity, Mary's sons (*John* 19:26), were and are now the children of the Father, no longer slaves, but members of God's immediate family[55].

---

[53] See Fr. John A. Hardon, S.J.: "God the Author of Nature and the Supernatural Part Two: Creation as a Divine Fact Section Two: Supernatural Anthropology THESIS VIII Before the Fall, Adam Possessed Sanctifying Grace and the Preternatural Gifts of Integrity, Immortality and Infused Knowledge".

[54] See Peter Ditzel, "When did the Old Covenant end and the New Covenant begin?", 2013.

[55] "So you are no longer a slave, but God's child; and since you are his child, God has made you also an heir". *Galatians* 4: 7.

Jesus' Father founded His New Covenant on Mary, "a woman who loves."[56] She was described "before all ages" thus:

> "How beautiful you are my love,
>
> How beautiful you are! [...]
>
> You are wholly beautiful, my love,
>
> And without a blemish."[57]

God's Covenant with Moses (*Exodus* 19-24) in Mount Sinai was founded on "fear of the Lord:" fear of breaking His Ten Commandments and fear of breaking His rules for everyday life. On the other hand, the New Covenant, made possible by Mary's pregnancy and Divine Maternity, was founded on Love. The New Covenant was made flesh by the Holy Spirit in Mary's womb. "God loves, and his love may certainly be called *eros*, yet it is also called *agape*."[58]

---

[56] Benedict XVI, *God is Love*, # 42.

[57] *Song of Songs*, 4, 1-7.

[58] Benedict XVI, *"God is Love"*, I. 9.

Mary brought Love into the world; she gave flesh to God's Word. The Virgin Mother made it possible for humanity to return to the Father's kingdom. The New Adam revealed His Father's will for His sons by the Virgin: "Mary has truly become the Mother of all believers." That universal motherhood mentioned by Pope Benedict XVI results from her "most intimate union with God, through which the soul is totally pervaded by Him."[59]

Present at the *Big Bang* and Present at the Annunciation.

Following Father George Lemaître, scientists continue to accept his *Big Bang* story, "the most beautiful theory of Creation", as Albert Einstein called it. Because the scientific method and other systems of acquiring knowledge apply only to things existing in time and space, *the "nature" of the original entity that exploded and created them remains a mystery*. To illustrate the logic of this learning impossibility (our understanding is limited to *temporal*

---

[59] Benedict XVI, *loc. cit.*

manifestations of the *eternally Present*) the example of death may be useful. We cannot know what death is, any more than we can know what caused the *Big Bang* and what was that exploded. Both death and that *Big Bang* occurred in the Present, i.e., before there were past and future, before time existed.

What no longer remains a mystery after the *Big Bang*, is the fact that it did happen. The explosion and everything that followed is the first and foremost act of revelation of the Mysterious Author that creates the Universe.

If we - scientists, priests, and all other human beings – accept the information our senses provide, and apply the logical demands of our intelligence to that information, we must conclude that Something or Some One was *Present* to trigger the explosion. *Big Bang* reveals the Creator is Present (i.e., timeless, eternal) in the beginning of time, now, and at the end of time, if there is such.

Prophets and Mary.

The word "prophets" refers to persons who seem to know the future. The importance and credibility of a prophecy is best evaluated by its consequences on the community which accepts it. The prophets themselves may recede from public notice or become subjects of public disbelief and even scorn: "Truly I tell you," he continued, "no prophet is accepted in his hometown." (*Luke* 4, 24).

Many prophets and events demonstrate that the same Creative Spirit is present in all of them. For example, Cosmic Evolution – the aftermath of Big Bang – cannot be explained absent a transcendent Love "that moves the Sun and the other stars."[60]

Because he is considered as the foundation of the predominant culture at the time of Jesus, Plato is a fine example among thousands who concluded that the execution of Love

---

[60] Last line of Dante's *Divina Comedia*.

creates man, and provides the energy to create. The name of this Omnipresent Eternal Spirit is Love:

> The worship of this god, he said, is of the oldest, for Love is unbegotten... Thus we find that the antiquity of Love is universally admitted and in very truth is the ancient source of all our highest good."
> (*Symposium*,178b-c).

In our own time, Pope Emeritus Benedict XVI once more confirmed the name of "the source of our highest good" in his beautiful encyclical *God is Love*.

Two thousand years ago a peasant girl from Nazareth was enlightened by her Lover's Spirit to change her religious culture, and to abandon the Mosaic Law of the Old Covenant. The Virgin Mary chose to do the will of her Lover, her God. Thanks to her total submission "to thy Word," she conceived the Son of God, her Lover and her Beloved. A new Creation began in her womb, a *novus ordo seclorum:* a New Covenant began with the Virgin's Son Jesus.

"But when the fullness of the time had come, God sent forth His Son, born of a woman, born under the law," Saint Paul would write to the Galatians (4: 4). During his lifetime, Mary's Son identified Himself with the Beginning and the End ($\Delta\Omega$), a.k.a., God, the $\Delta\Omega$ of All that is. In more familiar words, "through him all things were made." The time had come - the "fullness of time" - for the Mystery of Love to reveal Itself.

The girl from Nazareth began to reveal the Mystery of Love. and she herself became that revelation. It was not being religious, thinking logically, nor knowing history or philosophy that the Virgin Mary became the "*ancilla Domini*" (the Lord's servant). It was her unconditional surrender to her Lover's will that would make her "Theotokos", the mother of God:

"Mary, Virgin and Mother, shows us what
love is and whence it draws its origin and

its constantly renewed power." (*God is Love*, # 42).

Mary's role in *creating* the New Covenant required more than her understanding and her will, however essential these characteristics were to her personality. Mary's Divine Lover – *Eros* - required her body as well, the total person:

> "For us men and for our salvation he came down from heaven, and by the Holy Spirit was incarnate of the Virgin Mary, and became man."

From that moment, it pertains to their Divine Son to reveal the identity of His Mother's Lover, His Father and how we are now and forever related to Him.

> "The Greeks—not unlike other cultures—considered *eros* principally as a kind of intoxication, the overpowering of reason by a "divine madness" which tears man

away from his finite existence and enables him, in the very process of being over-whelmed by divine power, to experience supreme happiness... *Eros* was thus cele-brated as divine power, as fellowship with the Divine." (*God is Love*, #4).

Sex: Natural and Supernatural.

In such sexual experiences, the two become one body thanks to the creative power of Love:

"This is why a man leaves his father and his mother and joins himself to his wife, and they become one body" (*Gen.* 2: 24).

At the instant Mary consented to become the Mother of God's "only begotten Son", the word *life* no longer referred to the product of biological evolution alone, nor to a merely temporal phenomenon. By Mary's conception, the Eternal Father interjected Himself into human history; the miracle of God's incarnation took place literally in "the fullness of time." From that moment forward, *life* took on the new meaning revealed by Jesus:

- "I am the way and the truth and the life;"
- "In him was life, and that life was the light of men;
- "Jesus said to her, 'I am the resurrection and the life. He who believes in me will live, even though he dies;'"
- "...his Son Jesus Christ. He is the true God and eternal life." (John 14, 6; 11, 25; 5, 20 respectively).

In the New Covenant, Life is Jesus Himself. It is also revealed that the Incarnation of God is "the primary end of the family." We are to provide the material means to manifest God among us, Emmanuel. To *turn over completely to God instead of Moses* was *the Virgin Mary's revolution*. Her Son implemented it, restoring us to our original supernatural existence: The Father welcomes us back into the Kingdom.

Jesus Himself gives true and valid meaning to the term "life" every time we find it in the *Catechism of the Catholic Church,* specifically in Article 6 , Part Three, chapter III, "The Love of Husband and Wife."

Quoting Pope John Paul II, *C.C.C.* # 2361 confirms that

> "Sexuality [...] is not something simply bio-logical, but concerns the innermost being of the human person as such. It is realized in a truly human way *only* if it is an integral part of the love by which a man and a woman commit themselves totally to one another until death." (*Familiaris Consortio,* # 11).

Other references in the *Catechism* reiterate Jesus' message of Love as the ultimate reason for our life and its sexual manifestations. The following numerals provide a clearer insight into the meaning of their content when the "procreation of life" is understood as the procreation of Jesus, of "God-is- with-us;"

C.C.C. #2332: "Sexuality affects all aspects of the human person in the unity of his body and soul. It specially concerns affectivity, the capacity to love and to procreate, and in a more general way the aptitude for forming bonds of communion with others."

C.C.C. #2337: "[...] Sexuality, in which man's belonging to the bodily and biological world is expressed, becomes personal and truly human when it is integrated into the relationship of one person to another, in the complete and lifelong mutual gift of a man and a woman."

C.C.C. #2361: "Sexuality, by means of which man and woman give themselves to one another through the acts which are proper and exclusive to spouses, is not something simply biological, but concerns the innermost being of the human person as such. It is realized in a truly human way only if it is an integral part of the love by which a man and woman commit themselves totally to one another until death" (*Familiaris Consortio*).

C.C.C.# 2367: quoted earlier, called to give life, spouses share in the creative power and fatherhood of God. '

These and other passages deserve special attention for their proper interpretation according to Jesus' Covenant of Love:

> "I give you a new commandment: love one another; just as I have loved you, you also must love one another. By this love, you have for one another, everyone will know that you are my disciples." (*John* 13, 34)).

C.C.C. # 2337 reaffirms that after the "only begotten Son of God [...] by the Holy Spirit was incarnate of the

Virgin Mary and became man," sexuality becomes *truly human* when integrated to an *interpersonal* relationship. Since we are created in God's image, that relationship reflects the "life" of the Trinity.

The last part of the numeral, i.e. "the complete and life-long mutual gift of a man and a woman," introduces gender into the sexual relationship. This contradicts the concept of "human person" as the unity of body and soul and *as the image of our (genderless) Creator.*

C.C.C. # 2361 emphasizes the mutuality of complimentary sexuality once again. The *sacrament* of marriage is one in which a man and a woman give themselves to one another. In this sacramental context, the *Catechism* reiterates the *spiritual* dimension of human sexuality: "it is realized in a truly human way *only* if it is an integral part of the love...."

Of the numerals mentioned here, #2367 lends itself to a materialistic interpretation of the purpose of human sexuality, the procreation of children. The life to which

The Catechism refers, however, is "not something simply biological," as Pope John Paul II wrote in *Familiaris Consortio*. The "creative power and fatherhood of God" are not revealed in the evolutionary process He created billions of years ago. It is only in the Eternal Present, that God's miracles occur.

"Cooperating with the love of God the Creator" is not a material, physical enterprise but simply another dimension of the single reality that is Love. *Married couples, single persons, consecrated virgins, celibate persons, heterosexuals and homosexuals, in sum, all of us, should regard as our "proper mission, to transmit human life," which we know by faith to be the life of Christ.*

Pleasure, a Dimension of Love.

"For I was afraid that you would answer my prayer at once and cure me too soon of the disease of lust..." (St. Augustine, *Confessions* VIII, 7). Today, St. Augustine's prayer could be that of a Christian Scientist. Once he overcame his Manichean past, Augustine would explain that lust is a *spiritual* affliction. If left uncontrolled by our intellect and our free will, that affliction can have *physical* consequences considered *sins* by most Christians. In those cases, lust becomes Lucifer's lure.

On the other hand, if the initial temptation of lust is controlled through prayer, Jesus will render Lucifer powerless, as He did after forty days in the desert. Thanks to the creative power of God the Father, the natural physical attraction of two human beings will be transformed into a supernatural spiritual act of Divine Love.

PART II

LOVE'S PRODIGAL SONS

Mary's bodily survival ensured the supernatural birth of her Son's Mystical Body

N*atural*, *supernatural*, *preternatural*: three words whose meanings have been discussed since the beginnings of Christianity[61]. Because believers fail to comprehend these words intimately and subjectively, Mary's role in their lives is frequently reduced to folkloric superstitions and popular customs that lead them away from her Son. The estrangement of the Virgin Mother from the Church after Pentecost remains in force today. Superstitious beliefs and pietistic practices fabricated around her, often

---

[61] See Fr. John A. Hardon, S.J., "God the Author of Nature and the Supernatural."

distract and separate the faithful from her Son's Mystical Body. A visit to Fatima, Lourdes, Mexico City, and hundreds of other places, illustrates how Mary's messages are relegated to the back of the minds of those who believe her story. Regarding Mary's apparitions, the hierarchy of the Church succeeded in

- making miracles the center of attraction and devotion, rather than her Son Jesus as she intended [62];

- Industrializing and commercializing the believers' devotional practices[63]; and

---

[62] Ex. gr., Saint John Paul II's explanation for surviving the attempt on his life: **"One hand fired the shot. Another (the hand of the Virgin Mary) guided it."** As a measure of his gratitude, John Paul gave the bullet that was extracted from his abdomen to the shrine; the bullet today forms part of the crown of the statue of the Virgin of Fatima." In http://www.michaeljournal.org/articles/roman-catholic-church/item/the-pope-of-our-lady-of-fatima See also: "The Miracle of the Sun was the greatest miracle since the Resurrection and points to the crucial importance of the message given by our Lady," in Guadalupe, Fatima, And Catholic Culture November 22, 2016 by Donald Anthony Foley, *The Wanderer.*

[63] For example, "Representative Ryan Zinke (R, MT) was nominated by Donald J. Trump to be the Secretary of the Interior. And at his Senate confirmation hearing, Rep. Zinke wore something unusual: socks with Our Lady of Gudalupe imprinted on them." http://churchpop.com/2017/01/18/trump-nominee-wears-our-lady-of-guadalupe-socks-to-confirmation-hearing/

- keeping the New Eve's messages away from the new Adam, i.e., the Mystical Body of Jesus.[64]

Jesus' disciples have analyzed the terms "natural", "supernatural", and "preternatural," since day one of the Church, i.e., since Pentecost. It was then that they experienced the creative and transformative power of the Spirit of Jesus.

After His resurrection, Christ's mission on Earth was coming to its end. It had begun some three decades earlier, when Mary consented to be the mother of God's Son. As had happened during the Annunciation, at Pentecost the Holy Spirit again came to Mary. The power of the Most

---

[64] "The probability lies within the realm of "extraordinary" phenomena, i.e., they are not common every day occurrences. *The credibility and authenticity of any particular apparition lies within the singular parameter of the hierarchical authority of the Church"*, in Marian Apparitions, by John Trigilio, http://www.ewtn.com/library/MARY/MEDJUGO.htm (emphasis added).

For example, "Representative Ryan Zinke (R, MT) was nominated by Donald J. Trump to be the Secretary of the Interior. And at his Senate confirmation hearing, Rep. Zinke wore something unusual: socks with Our Lady of Gudalupe imprinted on them." http://churchpop.com/2017/01/18/trump-nominee-wears-our-lady-of-guadalupe-socks-to-confirmation-hearing/

High covered her with the fires of Divine Love: this time she conceived her Son's Mystical Body. The birth of the Church, like that of Jesus, was a *supernatural* event that transcended the *natural* limitations of all who were present.

As He did with Adam, the Creator also endowed His Son's followers with *preternatural* gifts, indicating that Jesus' Church, the new-born Israel, would include all of humanity. "Some, however [ignoring the *supernatural* manifestations of the event], laughed it off. 'They have been drinking too much new wine, they said", attributing their newly found ability to speak in diverse tongues to *natural* causes like alcohol (*Acts*, 2).

This dichotomy, natural /supernatural, contributed to their confusion. Were they Jews, followers of Moses? Some were speaking Greek, others Latin, even languages from distant lands: what was their ethnic identity? *Naturally*, judging from their languages, they should be identified as Greeks, Romans, Persians, and from as far away as India or Egypt. The ability to "speak in tongues," however, was a *supernatural* gift. Those who received this gift, now belonged to the *supernatural* "kingdom" of God on Earth, "Emmanuel", conceived in the Virgin's womb.[65] The birth of the Christian Church, just like that of Jesus, constituted a *supernatural* phenomenon unique in the history of mankind.[66]

The apostle Peter tried to clarify the confusion of the "men of Judaea, and all you who live in Jerusalem" (*Acts*, 2; 14). He attested that his brothers and friends were not drunk. Peter identified all of them, as well as "the whole House of Israel," as followers of "this Jesus...both Lord and Christ" (*Acts*, 2; 36).

Were Jesus to ask his disciples today, "But who do you say I am?" (*Mark*, 8, 29), Peter's answer, "You are the

---

[65] "Her role in relation to the Church and to all humanity goes still further. "In a wholly singular way she cooperated by her obedience, faith, hope, and burning charity in the Savior's work of *restoring supernatural life to souls*. For this reason, she is a mother to us in the order of grace." *Catechism*, # 968. Emphasis added.

[66] The flames over their heads, the sounds "like a powerful wind from heaven," and the intimate experience of the presence of the Holy Spirit, undoubtedly were signs of a *supernatural* event.

Messiah," would not be satisfactory. More likely than not, Peter would have to say something like this:

"As a product of Darwinian evolution, i.e., *naturally*, you are a man, the son of Mary. But no one has seen your father. Therefore, we'll never know exactly who you are."

Could this double paternity mystery – Jesus' Father and Our Father - be resolved today? Applying a genetic test, for example? Such tests would prove fruitless: Mary's story clearly denies the presence and need of a male in the conception of Jesus. And, as Mary might have said in her old age, she enjoyed the "satisfaction which comes from the certainty that I will not say anything that is not true."[67]

Peter's answer, "You are the Messiah", appeals to a *supernatural* dimension whose existence is unknown to the apostle at that moment.[68] This dimension *cannot be*

---

[67] Colm Toibin, *The Testament of Mary*, Scribner, 2012; p. 2.

[68] *Matthew* 16, 16-18: "…it was not flesh and blood that revealed this to you but my Father in heaven."

perceived naturally, consequently, it cannot be proved scientifically. The evolution of Nature does not produce anything above or different from the merely *natural.* The defining characteristics of humans - intellectual activity and will power - do not result from the natural evolution of their bodies. *These characteristics emanate from the same Spiritual Force[69] that energizes the natural evolutionary processes of the Cosmos.* The source of that force is found in the *supernatural* dimension of the Cosmos.[70] Different cultures have called this transcendental source by various names at different times: Atman-Brahman (Hindus), the Immovable Spot (Buddha), Allah (Islam), YWH (Israel), and, among the followers of Jesus Christ, the Holy Spirit.

---

[69] "At the smallest and largest levels, we witness a kind of cosmic '*eros*,' an attraction of opposites written into the very design of the universe […] It's the code that God has written into the very order of things – the 'divinity code' -shall we say;" Christopher West, *Fill These Hearts, God, Sex, and the Universal Longing*, Image, page 90.

[70] "Through him all things came to be, not one thing had its being but through him. All that came to be had life in him…" *John* I, 3-4.

73

Mary's Motherhood.

The fertilization of an egg does not always begin a chain reaction resulting in a human being. The material components of aborted babies differ from those in corpses only in quantity and age. However, a dead baby and a corpse share one characteristic in common: neither can restart the chain reactions that began their lives on its own . A live human being begins life when and if an *immaterial* dynamism *animates* the chemicals present in a fertilized egg.[71] That immaterial force is *not natural* to the matter in human bodies, if it were, persons would be animated for as long as the life-sustaining materials remained in them: whoever has witnessed anyone's death can attest to the contrary.

The source of animation, the soul, is not found in Nature. *Animation* of matter is *super* (above) *natural*. The Creator of Nature breathes *His own life* into the fertilized

---

[71] If a chain of changes begins in the new entity (i.e., the fertilized egg), it will be thanks to the supernatural Omnipotent Creative Love, and not to the spermatozoid and the egg which no longer exist.

egg; only then does human life begin[72].

The Virgin Mary, the Breath of God and the Reproduction of Love.

Mary's story tells of a *virginal* conception, in which the *supernatural* Creative Power of God's Love, substituted for the absent *natural* factors (spermatozoids) necessary for physical conception. For "nothing is impossible for God". The Holy Spirit, "the breath of God", as Gordon P. Robertson[73] translates *pneuma*, breathed its Divine Life into Mary, the New Eve, and she conceived Jesus.[74]

---

[72] "Human life is sacred because from its beginning it involves the creative action of God and it remains forever in a special relationship with the Creator, who is its sole end. God alone is the Lord of life from its beginning until its end: no one can under any circumstance claim for himself the right directly to destroy an innocent human being." *C.C.C.*, # 2258, quotes "The Gift of Life", *Donum Vitae*, Intro., 5.

[73] Gordon P. Robertson, C.E.O. of the Christian Broadcasting Network, offers an elegant synthesis of the meanings of nouns and phrases relevant to the Pentecost event; see www.cbn.com/700club/holy-spirit-breath-god

[74] "At the end of this mission of the Spirit, Mary became the Woman, the new Eve ('mother of the living'), mother of the 'whole Christ'." *Catechism*, # 726.

C.C.C. # 733 to 747 explain the role of "God's gift" to humanity, Divine Love. *C.C.C.* # 744 summarizes this sub-section on the Reproduction of Love:

> "In the fullness of time, the Holy Spirit completes in Mary all the preparations for Christ's coming among the People of God. By the action of the Holy Spirit in her, the Father gives the world Emmanuel, 'God-with-us'" (*Mt* 1:23)."

As was stated earlier, "The fullness of time" is "Now", the ever-present Present, as opposed to the ever-gone Past and the not-yet Future.[75]

The Present *is* the fullness of time: the totality of time past brings us the Present, the eternal "Now." Note the following:

1) In the Judeo-Christian tradition, God identifies Himself with the Present: "I am who I Am...This

---

[75] "The future is the least real of the three dimensions of time," Peter J. Kreeft, *I Burned For Your Peace*, Ignatius Press, 2016; page 144.

is my name for *all time*" (*Exodus*,3, 14-15). Jesus also identified Himself with the Present: "Before Abraham was born, I Am" *John*, 8: 58.

2) Intelligence and Free Will operate exclusively in the Present, i.e., *in* "I AM". Whenever we apply our intelligence exclusively to facts, i.e., things that *were*, we risk confusing facts with *what is*, now (Reality).

3) The Expression of God's Omnipresent Love (a.k.a. "Creation") is ever Present, whether humans are aware of it or not.

Everyone's earthly life begins at conception and evolves in time and space. What we *are* does not evolve[76]. We *are what we are* only and always in the (ever-present) Present: a Reality that *is,* does not become. Who and what we and the Omnipresent Creator are now, is constantly revealed in time and space. Each of us (I and God) *is*, only

---

[76] This apparent paradox recalls Plato's quote attributed to Heraclitus "'No man ever *steps in the same river twice,* for it's not the *same river* and he's not the same man.' (Cratylus 402, a).

in the Present. Who we are is revealed *in* and *by* I AM; as it was revealed to the apostle Peter[77]. *Who I am* is NOT in the past nor in the future.[78]

---

[77] Matthew 16:17.

[78] Paul Tillich's *The Eternal Now*, Charles Scribner's Sons, NY, 1963, and Saint Augustine's *Confessions,* Book XI are basic readings on this topic.

All artists give life to their creations, their own.

Chapter 2:

The Authority of the Supernatural Author

"The artist, like the God of the creation, remains within or behind or beyond or above his handiwork..." James Joyce.[79]

Most humans have not evolved sufficiently to appreciate, in just measure, their kinship to their Creator. This existential lapse does not result from "natural" causes found in Cosmic Evolution. A glance at the most recent comprehensive version of the creation of the Cosmos will help understand the meanings of those two terms, *natural* and *supernatural*. The concept of Authority will be elucidated as well.

---

[79] *Portrait of the Artist as a Young Man*, Penguin, 1964, page 215.

Father George Lemaitre's *Big Bang* Theory (1927 AD) places the beginning of Creation some 14 to 17 billion years ago. The theory states that an explosion initiated the expansion of the Universe in which we live.[80] The origin of the compressed "spiral nebula" or the "primeval atom" that exploded giving birth to Creation, remains a mystery. An intelligent analysis of the mythical *Big Bang* Theory indicates an immaterial, *uncreated* source of energy. Such a spiritual or immaterial dimension of existence necessarily postulates a spiritual Author of Being, capable of "authoring" being (of creating) of its own accord.

Rather than accepting (and adopting) the supernatural identity the Virgin Mary provided us, that of being her Son's brothers and sisters, we continue living *naturally*, as mere animals, albeit if "rational". Thus, the refusal

---

[80] "... the matter of the spiral nebulae was compressed into a relatively restricted space, at the time the cosmic processes had their beginning". Pius XII, Address to the Pontifical Academy of Sciences, November 22, 1951, # 36.

to acknowledge the supernatural (metaphysical) origins[81] of authority and sexuality has hindered the evolution of mankind. Our estrangement from our Creator is the consequence of deliberate choices NOT to transcend ourselves and our time and space.

<u>Authority and Sexuality.</u>

In regards to the concepts of authority and sexuality, humans have made little progress beyond that brought about by the Evolution of Nature. Instead of exercising authority, humans developed physical and material characteristics that allowed the mature males to dominate and oppress their weaker counterparts, females, infants and the elderly.

In the animal kingdom, Alpha males control their territory and protect their group's weaker members by the use of physical power. Such use and abuse of physical power prevails today, despite the essential modification Biological Evolution produced 100,000 to 200,000

---

[81] "… all things find in You (God) their origin…" St. Augustine quotes *Rom.* II,30 in his *Confessions*, I, 2.

years ago, when *homo sapiens* appeared on Earth. Then, *wisdom,* was made accessible to humanity: intelligence transcended the merely intuitive knowledge of the rest of the animal kingdom. Intuition and emotional learning depend on and are limited by the matter that makes up the various systems of perception, i.e,. the senses and their physiological instruments. The evolutionary process prepared the matter of the human brain to transcend its limitations. For example, one's sight uses the eyes, the optic nerve, and a region of the brain that perceives what exists outside that sense. Human intelligence transcends the material components of the senses to create an *immaterial* concept of what was seen in that person's soul; for example, the concept of beauty.

Mere biological evolution does not provide the brain with the spiritual ability to transcend itself; this would constitute circular reasoning, like a creator creating Itself. Endowed with the necessary mechanisms to perceive and conceptualize spiritual aspects of reality, humans can read[82] the material signs provided by the senses. We know the real things behind sensorial appearances by *under-standing*[83] or substantiating their perceived appearances.

What do souls do?

Human intelligence and will power are found in everyone's spirit or soul. Insofar as these spiritual instruments rely on the brain and other material mechanisms of the body, they are bound by time and space. Each soul *animates*[84] a specific quantity of matter.[85] Animation of matter occurs only *in the Present, not in the past nor in the future.* *SPIRIT*

Our intelligence and our desire to understand, impel us to find the foundation of our bodily existence, i.e., of our lives. At one time or another, everyone wanders: "Who do you say

---

[82] "Intelligence", from Latin, *intus* and *legere*: "into" and "to read" respectively.

[83] "Under" and "standing", *sub* and *stans* in Latin: hence "substance."

[84] From the Latin *anima*, meaning "soul".

[85] "Designated matter" in Thomas Aquinas.

that I am?" (*Luke* 9, 20).[86] Only human beings can ask such a question and only human beings can answer it.

Our identity, who we are, now and forever, is revealed by the Author of "All-there-is", in the time and space where He is always Present. Our Maker, our Author, brings us to life in His Present, using matter He "authorized" to evolve in time and space. God is always Present; from the "Big Bang" instant, throughout Cosmic Evolution, to Now. He is the omnipresent Author of what and *in* Whom we are[87]. All authors create out of love, *ex amore creaturae*.

As it happens with the rest of humanity, Mary's supernatural identity is revealed in time and space. When Mary accepts God's invitation to become the Mother of His only begotten Son, His supernatural messenger reveals who she is. No longer "the handmaiden of the Lord," as she called

---

[86] We may well join St. Augustine: "I do not know where I came from when I was born into tis life which leads to death…"in *Confessions*, I, 6.

[87] In St. Augustine's words: "Surely, we can only derive them [our life and our very existence] from our Maker, from you, Lord, to whom living and being are not different things […but] are one and the same," *Confessions*, I,6.

herself, Mary becomes the mother of Emmanuel, "God among us". This supernatural identity does not come to the Virgin Mary from "flesh and blood," but from Our Father in heaven, now present in her womb (*Matthew* 16; 16-17).

"This is perhaps what we should expect when we consider that a work of creation is a work of love, and that love is the most ruthless of all the passions, sparing neither itself, nor its object, nor the obstacles that stand in its way."[88]

CHAPTER 3:

Through Mary, Love creates and restores all

"The woman brought a male child into the world, the son who was to rule all the nations with an iron scepter," *Revelation*.

The apostle Peter identified Mary's Son as the Messiah. The "New Eve" was the mother of God's only begotten Son. Thirty some years later, at the climax of His Father's Redemptive Act of Love, Jesus makes us His Divine Mother's sons: "He said to his mother, 'Woman,

---

[88] Dorothy L. Sayers, *The Mind of the Maker*, Living Age Books, 1956, p. 127.

JOHN

this is your son.' Then, to the disciple, He said, 'This is your Mother.'[89]

From His cross, instants before dying, Jesus Christ brings all humans back to His Father. We are restored to our original supernatural condition as sons of Mary, "children of God"." Since Pentecost, the children of God became the Mystical Body of Jesus Christ: we are now *in* "I AM," we transcend time and space. The Author of "All-there-is", the Omnipresent Love, creates our timeless soul[90] to function in our time-bound, bodies.[91] Whenever God *in-forms* matter with a human soul, He begets Emmanuel, God among us.

All creations are products of the love of their creators, human or Divine. In the latter cases, because the Creator is One, the Creative Love that creates "All-there-is," does so

---

[89] *John* 19:26.

[90] "Before I formed you in the womb I knew you;" *Jeremiah*, 1:5

[91] "Our soul is as much in time as our body. Of itself, it is in spiritual time (*kairos*), and by being... the life of the body, it is also subject to material time (*kronos*)," in Kreeft, page 142.

in one and the same act[92]. "All-there-is," variously called Creation, the Cosmos, the Universe, and Nature, contains all that exists, including other [possible] universes. The Divine Creator is One and so is His Creation.

On the other hand, human creators are infinite in number, as are their creations. An artist's creation is as perfect, as beautiful, as true to life, and as good, as she or he can make it. If humans were true creators, and not mere re-arrangers of existing matter, they could endow their creations with a life of their own, as the Greek myth of Pygmalion suggests. Speaking of artistic creations, the Russian artist Wassily Kandinsky (1866-1944) wrote that

> "The work of art is born of the artist in a mysterious and secret way. *From him it gains life and being.*"[93]

---

[92] "Let there be light and there was light: 'tis so:/For was, and is, and will be, are but is;/And all creation is one act at once, /" in A. Tennyson, "The Princess; A Medley." Part iii.

[93] Wassily Kandinsky, *Concerning the Spiritual in Art*, Dover Publications, 1977, page 53, emphasis added.

But since *no mere human* creator can claim to be "Life"[94], no human creator can truly give it to her/his creatures.

Human creations transcend their makers.

The talented *human* artist breathes his own "life" into his/her artistic creations. Both lives - that of the art as well as that of the artist - are limited in time and space. However, the artist's soul, always *in* Present, can and does breathe its being to his work. In other words, a human act of creation is an image of the Divine act of Creation: both "breathe" life into their creatures. Human art enjoys human "life", Divine art enjoys Divine Life. The *spirit* of the human maker will be present in his/her art for as long as its materials last. The spirit of the Divine Maker is present in His art in Eternity.

Whether the works we perceive in *our* own days are ancient, modern, or contemporary, the fact that they bring

---

[94]See *John* 11:25 and 14:6.

GONZALO T. PALACIOS

Beauty, Truth, Goodness, and Being to our Present, means that they transcend and transform us and their makers[95].

The Creator breathes His Own Life into His Creation, into "All-there-is". It is a Life that *animates* the Universe and is always Present in it. The life of Divine Art – Creation and human beings - transcends its temporal components[96]. For Divine Art to be and to exist, it must be perceived by the Artist Himself, *always Present* in His works[97]. Our Divine Creator is perfect and omnipotent: humans are created in His image. When we are brought into the world, we manifest our Divine Creator, whether we are aware of doing so or not.

---

[95] N.B., The word "poet" in Greek – ποιητής, - means maker, doer, performer.

[96] "The word of Yahweh was addressed to me, saying, 'Before I formed you in the womb I knew you;'" *Jeremiah*, I, 4.

[97] "Through Him all things were made [born of the Father before all ages]", Nicene Creed. The Eternal Presence of God in His Creation constitutes what is called "Divine Providence".

Mary and the Authority from our Author.

We humans, and all of Creation, owe our eternal being to our Eternal Author, and our existence, being here and now, to our parents and our Common Author. Our soul recognizes that Author in the *person* each of us is, "a unified creature composed of body and soul, who loves;"[98] optimally exemplified by the Virgin Mary. God is Love and He is our *Author, the source of all Authority.* Love is the Supernatural Authority that enables us to transcend our physical nature and to recognize It in ourselves. When Mary became the Mother of God, we were raised to our original supernatural existence. Thus, we are now sons of the Virgin Mary, brothers of Jesus Christ, as He confirmed it at His Crucifixion. For the Omnipotent, Omnipresent Father of Jesus, "*nothing is impossible*".[99] *God the Father knew the Mystical Body of his only begotten Son, i.e., the Church, before forming Him in Mary's womb.* Thanks to

---

[98] *God is Love*, # 5.

[99] *Luke*, I, 38.

our Blessed Mother, the Incarnation of the Word of God revealed the definitive identity of each human being. We share Our Maker's Divinity:

> "For by His incarnation the Son of God has united Himself in some fashion with every man."[100]

---

[100] Paul VI, *"De Ecclesia in Mundo Huius Temporis"*, a.k.a., *The Church Today,* Documents of Vatican II, Rome, December 7, 1965; Part I, Chapter 1, # 22. Jesus made it possible for us to experience this eternal union at the Last Supper.

"So Yahweh God expelled him
From the garden of Eden."

CHAPTER 4:

Mary's restoration of humanity and of Creation to their original supernatural state.

"" But it was only right we should celebrate
and rejoice, because your brother here was
dead and has come to life; he was lost and
is found."

erhaps the most significant revelation God made about humanity through the Virgin Mary, was that of her Immaculate Conception. She was conceived and brought into the world completely free of sin, without blemish to obscure her love for her Maker: this is the essence of the dogma of the Immaculate Conception. But, what came first: Mary's Immaculate Conception or the Incarnation of her

Divine Lover's Son? Or, were those two events preceded by Jesus' sacrifice that restored humanity and Creation to their original sinless condition?[101] These questions would imply that God's actions are those of a creator bound by time. God, however, is not in time but in the Eternal Present, and His Creation is "one act at once."[102] The order of the world (κόσμος) is not sequential in Eternity: "the human mind, in this life, is utterly powerless to form a positive notion of eternity."[103]

"The most significant revelation God made about humanity", alludes to the dogma of Mary's Immaculate Conception in Eternity and to the restoration of Creation to

---

[101] See *Genesis*, I, 31: "God saw all he had made, and indeed it was very good:" Adam and Eve spoiled and lost the Divine Goodness God had imparted on His Creation and its creatures. "…the penalty alone was voluntarily assumed by the Redeemer and, in paying it, He washed away our sins and restored us to our former supernatural state and destination," *Catholic Encyclopedia*, "Redemption", subsection Satisfaction of Christ. See also, Aquinas, *Summa Theologiae*, III, 1.

[102] See Note 24, above. Saint Augustine had said in more accurate terms: "The works of the Trinity are indivisible…" in *On the Trinity*, 1.

[103] Avery Cardinal Dulles, SJ, in *Newman*, referring to his *Grammar of Assent*.

its original condition in Paradise. *As sons and daughters of Mary, the sinless New Eve, and of her Divine Lover, we are also conceived free of sin. Neither parent of Jesus' Mystical Body could pass on the original sin of Adam and Eve.*

Our Lord's sacrifice at Golgotha had eternal effects that transcended time and space. His words on the Cross ("this day you shall be with me in Paradise"), His descent into Hell ("the dead will hear the voice of the Son of God"),[104] His Resurrection, and the events that followed until his Ascension to Heaven, clearly show Him in Eternity, no longer in earthly time and space. Saint Thomas Aquinas summarized this Eternal Truth in these words:

> "He washed away our sins and restored us to our former supernatural state and destination."[105]

---

[104] *C.C.C. # 635; Jn* 5: 25.

[105] See Note 30.

Were this not the case, and humanity was not restored to its original sinless condition, there would be no Christianity today, and the Mystical Body would not exist. Had Mary been conceived and born in original sin, the Annunciation ("The Lord is with you," *Luke* 1, 26) would not have taken place. But it did take place; and "Mary believed the message of the angel and by her obedience brought about the redemption of the human race."[106] Mary's Immaculate Conception prepared her to be "*Mater Creatoris* (Mother of Our Creator)", "*Mater Salvatoris*, (Mother of Our Savior)," "Queen of the Prophets," and other titles with which the faithful have always addressed her. The "faithful" comprise those who believe Jesus meant it when he told his apostle John, "Behold your Mother."

Mary's Immaculate Conception, her Divine pregnancy out of human wedlock, her being "full of grace", and her ability to communicate through time and space with her

---

[106] Dulles, *Newman*, page 77.

children[107]: none of this could happen unless Our Lord's sacrifice at Golgotha had timeless, eternal effects. Mary's life began with her sinless conception, in the Eternity of the Present, in I AM. And, in the Eternal Present, slightly over two thousand years ago, she was assumed into Heaven (Eternity). Today the poor girl from Nazareth continues her Life in Him as the "Queen of Heaven".

---

[107] "Just as Eve was the 'mother of all the living' (Gen. 3:20), so Mary is the mother of all who live in the supernatural order of grace," Dulles, page 76.

"All visible creation, all the universe, bears the effects of man's sin". *Romans*, 8:22.

CHAPTER 5:

Mary and the Restoration of Creation[108]

"Blessed are the pure in heart, for they will see God."

Many religious writers have written about the sacredness of Creation. Those holy scriptures that survived the ravages of time, weather, and human destruction, all bear witness to religious beliefs relating to Cosmic Creation. Those myths, specifically those dealing

---

[108] For a more complete analysis of this topic, see Celia Deane-Drummond's excellent articles in http://biologos.org/blogs/archive/evolution-atonement-and-the-redemption-of-all-creation-part-1 and http://biologos.org/blogs/archive/evolution-atonement-and-the-redemption-of-all-creation-part-1#sthash.0AV6dlop.dpuf . Also, http://colossianforum.org/2015/09/04/evolution-atonement-and-the-redemption-of-all-creation-part-2/.

with Earth, usually refer to the existence and activities of one or more transcendental deities (i.e., monotheism or polytheism) who designed the Cosmos and everything in it[109].

In the Christian tradition, the plan of creation is a *grace, a* divine gift that establishes the human-to-God-to-human relationship called "religion". A harmonious coexistence with one's Creator and gratitude for Her[110] manifestations in Nature initially characterize most religions. However, whenever man's understanding of his surroundings and of himself fails him, the usual reaction is to blame God for his inability to comprehend God's signals.

Frequently, if not always, men do not understand why a gift from the gods like water becomes a curse like a tsunami. Rather than acknowledge the supernatural dimension of Creation where *natural* events must be interpreted

---

[109] For example: "I believe in one God. The Father almighty, maker of heaven and earth, of all things visible and invisible," opening of the Nicene Creed.

[110] The pronoun "she" refers to God as accurately as "he". "It" indicates other than a person: if applied to a "divinity", the pronoun "it" would indicate an idol.

supernaturally, humans judge them as mere catastrophes, in physical, materialistic terms.

The suffering that natural catastrophes cause to humans, however, does not entirely destroy their trust in the Creator. No suffering succeeds in breaking up the "human-to-God-to-human relationship" mentioned above. On the contrary, the "God-to-human" link of the relation is made stronger by the nurturing of Mother Nature, whose names include "Pachamama" (Mother Earth, Inca mythology), Pṛthvī Mātā (Hindu for Mother Earth), Gaea (Greek myth), and Terra (Roman myth). In the Christian culture, Mary, not a "goddess" but rather, a socially insignificant Jewish maiden, gives birth to and nurtures, the definitive "human-to-God" link, her Son Jesus.

Evolution brought about male physical power to the animals, supplanting female spiritual authorship (authority) and freedom of will. At this point, a brief explanation of the title of this essay, *Mary, the Unwed Mother of God*, is appropriate.

> ".. the rivers of mythology and philosophy run
> parallel and do not mingle till they meet in the

sea of Christendom." G. K. Chesterton, *The Everlasting Man*.

The myth of the Incarnation.[111]

One fundamental characteristic of God's definitive revelation, is His choice of meek and humble men and women to cooperate with His Son in the redemption of Creation. Jesus' early disciples were humble and, more importantly, politically powerless. Nineteen centuries later, Karl Marx might have called them the "Lumpenproletariat". This description fits many of His followers through the ages: Mary Magdalen, Francis of Assisi, Joan of Arc, Jean-Marie Vianney ("le cure d'Ars"), and Mother Teresa of Calcutta.

The Virgin Mary is the exemplar of Her Son's disciples. The Divine Lover chose her to beget His Son. She was from a poor village in Judea under absolute Roman domination.

---

[111] The word "myth" is used advisedly: it refers to a story or narrative used to express and reveal a mystery. Literature on this topic is extensive; Luis Cencillo's *Mito, Semántica y Realidad* (Madrid, 1970) is excellent. G. K. Chesterton's essay "Man and Mythologies" in *The Everlasting Man* gives a succinct but accurate account of the use of myths in Christianity.

Despite her circumstances, the young girl showed an independent spirit all her life[112]. The evangelists describe her as "full of grace," incapable of choosing any other than God, i.e., Love, above all things. She was following her Son's commandment three decades before He made it public.

Oppressive and arrogant persons are satisfied to be by themselves; they do not love anyone else. They do not know the gift (grace) of Love: they are *dis-graced*. The meek are free from material and physical shackles: they can love others unconditionally; mere love of self is not enough. In brief, those described in Jesus' beatitudes enter His kingdom of Love which "will have no end."

Why did God choose the Virgin Mary to conceive and give birth to Jesus? Why had she "won God's favor"? God had filled her with gifts – graces – that prepared her for Divine Maternity. At the height of His teaching, Jesus, like Moses,

---

[112] Doing God's will (as she understood it) instead of obeying the Mosaic Law and risking her own life and that of the Child in her womb, revealed an independent spirit, free from the strictest social restraints.

speaking to the crowds from a mount, revealed the Laws of
the New Covenant:

"Blessed are the poor in spirit, for theirs is the
kingdom of heaven.

[4] Blessed are those who mourn, for they will
be comforted.

[5] Blessed are the meek, for they will inherit
the earth.

[6] Blessed are those who hunger and thirst for
righteousness, for they will be filled.

[7] Blessed are the merciful, for they will be
shown mercy.

[8] Blessed are the pure in heart, for they will
see God.

[9] Blessed are the peacemakers, for they will
be called children of God.

[10] Blessed are those who are persecuted because
of righteousness, for theirs is the kingdom of
heaven. [11] "Blessed are you when people insult

you, persecute you and falsely say all kinds of evil against you because of me. [12] Rejoice and be glad, because great is your reward in heaven, for in the same way they persecuted the prophets who were before you" (*Matthew*, 5).

The Holy Spirit of Love would come upon the humble and powerless, not upon the arrogant and powerful. Great *is* their reward in Heaven, a.k.a. the Kingdom, where Jesus welcomed the Good Thief, a man who had broken at least the Tenth Commandment. The Law of Moses had been replaced by the Law of Christ: "I give you a new commandment:

Love one another;
Just as I have loved you,
You also must love one another'
By this love you have for one another,
everyone will know that you are my disciples.
John, 13; 34-35.

EPILOG

The Virgin Mary personified the Beatitudes, hers was the Kingdom of God. She dedicated herself to God totally, accepting to break the Mosaic Law to do His Will, and conceive His only begotten Son.

From the physical power and oppression found in Nature, Mary's *fiat* raised humanity to a supernatural life where God's authority and freedom prevail. This facet of Evolution – from Natural to Supernatural - took place in Mary's womb, energized by Love.

The following segments in the Book of Revelation allude to Mary's journey on Earth, ending in Heaven as Queen of Creation:

> "Now a great sign appeared in heaven: a woman, adorned with the sun, standing on the moon, and with the twelve stars on her

head for a crown. She was pregnant, and in labor, crying aloud in the pangs of child-birth. [...] and the dragon stopped in front of the woman as she was having the child, so that he could eat it as soon as it was born from its mother. The woman brought a male child into the world, the son who was to rule all the nations with an iron scepter, and the child was taken straight up to God and to his throne, while the woman escaped into the desert, where God had made a place of safety ready, for her to be looked after ...

[...] Then the dragon was enraged with the woman and went away to make war on the rest of her children, that is, all who obey God's commandments and bear witness for Jesus." *Revelation* 12: 1.

GLOSSARY

The following terms are defined solely as the author intended their meaning to be in the text.

Agape   Divine Love, God's love, manifested spiritually.

Animation   Gift of life, endowment of soul or spirit, in motion.

Authority   From "author", creator, maker; also, authorship.

Eros   Divine-human Love, manifested in the flesh, carnal.

Eternal   Not in time-space, the Present; Now, and forever.

Fantastic   Product of purely human fantasy, unreal existence.

Fiat   Latin, passive verb *fieri,* to be done; let it be done.

Immaterial   Spiritual, lacking matter.

Machismo   Male power. A *machista* is one who attributes overall superiority to the males of the species.

Myth   Story told to reveal the significance of a mystery; origins of myths are usually mysteries themselves.

Natural   Produced by Cosmic Evolution.

Power   The capability to control, oppress, and submit others by force and superior strength.

Preternatural Beyond the possible results of Cosmic Evolution'

Submission   Voluntary obedience to one's authority (see "Author").

Supernatural Related to preternatural; above and beyond natural.

Temporal   Passing from a yet non-existing future to a no-longer existing past. All temporality is provided by and sustained in Eternity (see above).

BIBLIOGRAPHY

A

Athanasius, "On the Incarnation of the Word," New Advent, Fathers of the Church. http://www.newadvent.org/

Aristotle, *On the Soul* (De Anima).

Aquinas, Thomas, *Summa Theologiae*, I-II, 3, q.29.

Augustine of Hippo, *Confessions*.
Homily # 7 on St. John's First Epistle, Paragraph 8.

B

Benedict XVI, *God is Love*, Encyclical, Rome 2005.
Jesus of Nazareth, 2007.

The Jerusalem Bible, 1966.

C

Catechism of the Catholic Church, 1994.

Chesterton, G. K., *The Everlasting Man,* 2007.

D

Dante, *The Divine Comedy*.

Davis, Emalon, "How the Incarnation did not limit the ubiquity of theWord... https://www.ccel/athanasius/incarnation.html

Deanne-Drummond, Celia, http://biologos.org/archive/evolution-atonement-and-the-redemption-of-all-creation-part-1

Ditzel, Peter, "When did the Old Covenant End and the New CovenantBegin?" 2013, wordofhisgrace.org

Dulles SJ, Avery Cardinal, "The Covenant with Israel," *First Things*,November 2005.

Newman, 2002.

F

Foley, Donald Anthony, "Guadalupe, Fatima, and Catholic Culture," *TheWanderer*, November 22, 2016.

H

Hardon, SJ, John A., "God the Author of Nature and the Supernatural"

J

Jourmet, Charles with Jacques Maritain, "On Human Sexuality,"*Theological Studies*, # 62, 2001.

Joyce, James, *Portrait of the Artist as a Young Man*, 1964.

John Paul II, Pope, *Familiaris Consortio*, 1994, Rome. *Prologue*, Catechism of the Catholic Church, 1994.

K

Kandinsky, Wassily, *Concerning the Spiritual in Art,* 1977.

Kreeft, Peter J., *I burned for your peace*, 2016.

L

Latz, Leo J., *The Rhythm*, 1942.

M

Merton, Thomas, *Love and Living*, 1981.

N

Newman, John Henry Cardinal, *An Essay on the Development ofChristian Doctrine*, 1878.

Apologia Pro Vita Sua, 1950.

O

Orth, Maureen, "The Virgin Mary, the World's Most Powerful Woman," *National Geographic*, December 2015.

P

Paul VI, Pope, "The Church in the Modern World", 1965 *Gaudium et Spes*.

Pius XII, Pope, "Address to Midwives", Rome 1951.

Plato, *The Symposium*.

R

Rahula, Walpola, L'enseignement du Bouddha d'après les textes les plusanciens, "L'Amour Universel," 1961.

Robertson, Gordon P.,

www.cbn.com/700club/holy-spirit-breath-god

Rockwell, Nancy, "No More Lying About Mary", *Patheos*, 12/03/2016.

Q

The Noble Qu' ram.

S

Sayers, Dorothy L., *The Mind of the Maker*, 1956.

T

Toibin, Colm, *The Testament of Mary*, 2012.

Tennyson, Alfred Lord, "The Princess, a Medley."

Tillich, Paul, *The Eternal Now*, 1963.

Trigillo, John, http://www.ewtn.com/library/mary/med-jugo.htm

W

West, Christopher, *Fill These Hearts, God, Sex, and the UniversalLonging*, 2012.

CPSIA information can be obtained
at www.ICGtesting.com
Printed in the USA
FFOW05n1839250617